Lewis and Clark's Bittersweet Crossing

by

Carol Lynn MacGregor

with illustrations by

Gaye Hoopes

CAXTON PRESS

2004

Library of Congress Cataloging-in-Publication Data
MacGregor, Carol Lynn, 1942-
  Lewis and Clark's bittersweet crossing / by Carol Lynn MacGregor ; illustrated by Gaye Hoopes.
      p. cm.
Summary: Describes the Lewis and Clark Expedition to explore the American West in the early 1800s, focusing particularly on the time the group spent with the Shoshoni and Nez Perce Indians in Idaho.
Includes bibliographical references.
  ISBN 0-87004-437-0 (alk. paper)
  1. Lewis and Clark Expedition (1804-1806)--Juvenile literature. 2. Lewis, Meriwether, 1774-1809--Relations with Indians--Juvenile literature. 3. Clark, William, 1770-1838--Relations with Indians--Juvenile literature. 4. Shoshoni Indians--Idaho--History--19th century--Juvenile literature. 5. Nez Perce Indians--Idaho--History--19th century--Juvenile literature. 6. Idaho--Description and travel--Juvenile literature. 7. West (U.S.)--Description and travel--Juvenile literature. [1. Lewis and Clark Expedition (1804-1806) 2. Lewis, Meriwether, 1774-1809. 3. Clark, William, 1770-1838. 4. Shoshoni Indians. 5. Nez Perce Indians. 6. Indians of North America--Idaho. 7. Idaho--Description and travel. 8. West (U.S.)--Description and travel.] I. Hoopes, Gaye. II. Title.
  F592.7.M237 2004
  917.804'2--dc22   2003017174

Lithographed and bound for
CAXTON PRESS
Caldwell, Idaho
170053

Printed in China

Thomas Jefferson's Dream

Thomas Jefferson dreamed about a trip over land to the Pacific Ocean for many years before the time was right for it to happen. When he became the third president of the United States in 1801, Jefferson brought Meriwether Lewis to Washington, D.C. to be his secretary. Lewis had grown up near Jefferson's home at Monticello. Jefferson prepared Lewis to lead an expedition west over land unknown to white men. Jefferson introduced Lewis to men who knew about astronomy, zoology, ethnology, botany, and medicine. With the training these men gave him, Lewis could describe birds, reptiles, fish, plants, and animals. He learned to write about the conditions, habits, and dress of native people he would meet. He also learned how to treat sick men and to use equipment to record exact locations in relation to the stars.

In January 1803, Jefferson asked Congress for secret funds for the trip. The land that the expedition would need to cross did not yet belong to the United States. Jefferson had sent Robert Livingston to Paris to buy the port of New Orleans. Fortunately, Napoleon Bonaparte, the leader of France, sold the United States all of "Louisiana," a large area of land including all the streams that fed the Missouri River. Nobody knew yet how far it was to the Continental Divide which separated the water that ran down the Missouri and Mississippi rivers into the Atlantic Ocean from water that flowed west to the Pacific Ocean. The Louisiana Purchase doubled the size of the United States. Lewis and Clark would explore this new territory.

In March 1804, the land in the Louisiana Territory became a legal part of the United States. There were only seventeen states then and the flag had only fifteen stars on it.

To prepare for the journey, Lewis ordered armaments at the U.S. Armory and Arsenal at Harper's Ferry, Virginia (now West Virginia). He wanted rifles, powder horns, tomahawks, knives, bullet molds, and repair kits for the guns.

After he became president of the United States, Thomas Jefferson hired his Virginia neighbor, Meriwether Lewis, as his private secretary. Jefferson introduced Lewis to many learned men to prepare him to lead an overland expedition to the Pacific Ocean. Here, they talk on the lawn at Jefferson's home, "Monticello," near Charlottesville, Virginia.

He also ordered a frame for an iron boat. In July, Lewis went to Pittsburgh to begin his trip down the Ohio River in a keelboat he had ordered made for the trip. He purchased a pirogue, a deep, long canoe that can hold a lot of baggage. He also bought a black Newfoundland dog named Seaman for $20, quite a sum in 1803.

The Jefferson peace medal was given to the chiefs of Indian tribes the explorers met during their travels.

On August 31, Lewis and several soldiers started the trip down the Ohio River from Pittsburgh. At Wheeling, Virginia (now West Virginia), he bought another, smaller pirogue. The river was very low, but Lewis managed to steer his keelboat down it. Seaman enjoyed swimming in the water.

Lewis recruited men along the way. He wanted practical, unmarried men used to working hard. He wanted men who would bring different talents to the group. These included Alexander Willard, a blacksmith; John Shields, a gunsmith; Patrick Gass, a carpenter; nine men from Kentucky who were good hunters and woodsmen, including the Field brothers, John Colter, and George Shannon, the youngest man at only nineteen. George Gibson proved to be an excellent fisherman. Nathaniel Pryor and Charles Floyd were cousins. Lewis appointed them to be sergeants. John Ordway was already a sergeant. The expedition was divided into three "messes" under these three leaders. The United States Army sponsored the expedition.

Lewis and his recruits arrived at Louisville, Kentucky, in October 1803, where they met William Clark. Lewis had known Clark several years before in the army. He respected and admired him, so he had asked Clark to share the leadership of a military expedition to explore the West. Clark agreed to share the command. He was a very friendly man who would make maps of western lands that are accurate even today. Even though the government did not give Clark the rank of captain that Lewis requested, no one on the expedition ever knew that. Lewis and Clark were in charge of the voyage together.

Clark brought his black slave, York, who had been with him all of his life. York experienced a freedom and independence on the expedition that few blacks in America at that time enjoyed. York carried his own gun, sometimes going on hunting trips apart from Clark. York delighted natives with his dancing and agility. They had never seen a black man, or such a large man so light on his feet.

On November 11, 1803, at Fort Massac, down the Ohio River near its confluence with the Mississippi River, Lewis

The expedition left Camp DuBois, near St. Louis, on May 14, 1804, heading up the Missouri River in a keelboat and two pirogues loaded with many supplies. Seaman, Lewis' dog, took the bow.

and Clark hired George Drouillard to be an interpreter. He was a Shawnee Indian whose father was at least half French. Although Drouillard did not know the languages of Indians the expedition would meet, he knew sign language and could communicate well with various tribes. He was a great hunter.

At the mouth of the Ohio River, the group turned north up the Mississippi River to the mouth of the Missouri River. They chose a site to spend the winter on the American side near present-day St. Louis. They called it Camp DuBois or Camp Wood. During the winter, the captains hired many French river boatmen to help get them up the Missouri River in the spring. At that time, there were no dams on the rivers. Melted snow from the Rocky Mountains made a lot of water that carried debris each spring. It took skilled men to steer watercraft around all of the debris and up the swift current.

 ## Up the Missouri

During the winter of 1803-1804, Lewis and Clark trained the men to follow military rules and discipline. The captains purchased provisions for the trip. They packed twenty-one bales of goods to trade with Indians, which included pipe tomahawks, tobacco, scissors, needles, mirrors, fish hooks, blankets, moccasin awls, beads, ribbons and handkerchiefs. In addition, they tried to take provisions they would need on the trip, such as bags of parchment, hulled corn, sugar, biscuits, coffee, beans and peas, barrels of flour and salt, kegs of pork and lard, boxes of candles, and many tools.

On May 14, 1804, they left Camp DuBois. The expedition then had two captains, three sergeants, eight corporals, twenty-four privates, an interpreter, a slave and about a dozen French river boatmen. French traders had been up and down this river for more than fifty years. The tribes along this route were used to seeing white people. The expedition soon met Kickapoo Indians and talked with Oto and Omaha Indians.

The journals tell us that in present-day Iowa Sergeant Charles Floyd became very ill and died, probably of appendicitis. In those days, there was no treatment for appendicitis. The members of the expedition voted to have Patrick Gass become sergeant in Floyd's place.

Several men were keeping journals, as President Jefferson had requested. Lewis, Clark, Ordway, Gass, Floyd, and

Whitehouse kept journals we can still read. Floyd's journal was, of course, short because he wrote from May until he died in August. Sometimes Lewis did not write. Whitehouse's journal stopped before the trip ended. Ordway wrote every day, and Gass and Clark wrote almost every day. Frazer wrote a journal, yet unfound. Perhaps there were others.

Lewis' drawing of a
native battle ax.

In present-day South Dakota, the Lewis and Clark Expedition met a French trader, Pierre Dorion, married to a Yankton Sioux woman and living at her village. Farther north, they had some trouble with the Lakota people (Teton Sioux), a very powerful tribe that wanted to control river traffic. Proceeding on, the expedition stayed with the Arikara tribe, where they shared entertainment by dancing and playing the fiddle as they usually did with Native Americans. They also gave political speeches, presented U.S. flags and Jefferson peace medals, and demonstrated Lewis' air gun that impressed natives as "big medicine."

They reached the Mandan and Hidatsa villages on the Knife River of present-day North Dakota in October 1804. They built a fort where they could live during the winter. It was extremely cold, but they enjoyed good relations with the Mandan and Hidatsa people in the area. They traded manufactured goods for food, especially corn. They hunted for meat.

At Fort Mandan, they hired Toussaint Charbonneau and his Shoshoni wife to be interpreters for the trip west in the spring. Her name was Sacagawea. A sixteen-year-old, she had a baby on February 11, 1805, named Jean Baptiste Charbonneau. About five years earlier, the Hidatsa people had stolen Sacagawea from her home in present-day Idaho. Later, she became one of Charbonneau's Indian wives.

Early in April, the ice broke up on the Missouri River, allowing boats to pass. All the corporals, one private and most of the French river boatmen returned to St. Louis in the keelboat. They took some caged animals and many samples of plants with them for President Jefferson. The rest of the party headed west up the Missouri. These thirty-three people have since been called "The Corps of Discovery."

Between the Mandan village and the Shoshoni homeland, the expedition didn't see any Native Americans. They did meet a number of animals, however, that were new to Euro-Americans. These included timber wolves, grizzly bears, elk, mule deer, diamond-backed rattlesnakes, cougars, antelope, and mountain sheep and goats.

During the winter, Hidatsa Indians had told Lewis and Clark that they would need to get horses from the Shoshoni

On January 1, 1805, William Clark wrote that sixteen men visited the first Mandan village, "for the purpose of Danceing, by . . . request of the Chiefs of that Village." He asked York, ". . . my black Servent to Dance which amused the Croud Verry much, and Somewhat astonished them, that So large a man should be active . . ." (*Thwaites* 1:243) Pierre Cruzatte played the fiddle while William Clark and the Mandans observed.

On August 12, 1805, Meriwether Lewis wrote, "McNeal had exultingly stood with a foot on each side of this little rivulet and thanked his god that he had lived to bestride the mighty and heretofore deemed endless Missouri." (*Thwaites* 2:335)

Indians to cross the "stoney mountains" (Bitterroot Mountains, or Northern Rocky Mountains). The leaders had asked the Charbonneaus to join them to help in this goal.

In what is now Montana, they came to a waterfall on the Missouri that the Hidatsa had told them about. It was an awesome sight. The men had to carry the boats around the series of five falls. Even though the men were young and tough, it took more than a month to carry their baggage around the falls. They had to build carts with wheels to pull the boats over the hills and ravines to reach the river above the falls. For two weeks during the portage, three men tried to fit animal hides over an iron frame Lewis had brought to make a boat. Unfortunately, they could not make it water-tight. (People are still looking for its remains around Great Falls, Montana.)

The Corps of Discovery traveled more than 3,000 miles before entering land that is now Idaho at Lemhi Pass. On July 22, 1805, Sacagawea recognized Beaverhead Butte, a landmark near her homeland. They left their canoes near present-day Three Forks, Montana. An advance party of four men went to scout for Sacagawea's people.

Meeting the Lemhi Shoshoni

Meriwether Lewis, John Shields, Hugh McNeal and George Drouillard entered the land that is now Idaho at Lemhi Pass, the present boundary between Idaho and Montana. The crest of those mountains forms the Continental Divide that separates water that runs east to the Atlantic Ocean from water that runs west to the Pacific Ocean. Near the little spring that comes out of the mountains on the east side, McNeal straddled the creek and thanked his god that he had reached the end of the Missouri River.

Lemhi Pass, 7,373 feet high, was the highest point of land that the expedition crossed. Shoshoni people who lived there later became known as the "Lemhi Shoshoni."

On August 13, 1805, the four men met three female Shoshonis (sometimes they were called Snake Indians), who were picking berries. Lewis gave two of them presents of pewter mirrors, face paint, and a moccasin awl. Drouillard gestured to have them bring the men of the tribe to them. Soon, sixty Shoshoni men on swift horses raced toward them. Lewis laid down his gun and walked to meet the warriors. The chief and two others dismounted and talked to the women. Then the chief met Lewis and put his left arm around Lewis' right shoulder, his left cheek on Lewis' left

On August 13, 1805, Lewis wrote, "A chief and two others. . . advanced and embraced me very affectionately in their way which is by puting their left arm over you[r] wright sholder clasping your back, while they apply their left cheek to yours and frequently vociforate the word *ah-hi-e, ah-he-e* that is, I am much pleased, I am much rejoiced." (*Thwaites* 2:339-340)

cheek and exclaimed, "Ah-hi-e! Ah-he-e!" which Lewis soon learned to mean, "I am much pleased! I am rejoiced!" These natives had never seen white people before, but they greeted them affectionately and took them to their camp where they entertained them nearly all night with music and dancing. The Shoshonis lived in lodges shaped like cones that were made of willows. They had very little to eat.

Lewis explained that a larger party was coming. Some of the Shoshonis were very afraid. When the day came to meet Clark, Lewis wore Chief Cameahwait's clothes and Cameahwait wore Lewis' clothes. That made the Shoshonis feel that they wouldn't be hurt by Clark's group of white men who were coming. Meanwhile, Drouillard killed a deer and offered most of it to the Shoshonis, who eagerly ate part of it without cooking it.

On August 17, Clark arrived with the rest of the group. When Sacagawea saw her people, she danced for joy. She recognized her friend, a girl who had escaped the Hidatsa when they both had been stolen. She recognized the chief, Cameahwait, as her brother. It was truly a wonderful homecoming for her! The sixteen Indians, who had been waiting with Lewis, sang as they led the explorers back to the Shoshoni camp. At camp, three Indian leaders embraced Clark and sat him on a white robe. One of them tied pieces of seashells in his hair. Since they lived in the mountains, they highly valued seashells. The Shoshonis took off their moccasins and smoked with bare feet, which was their way of showing sincerity. The Shoshonis arranged to take thirty horses to carry the expedition's baggage over the mountains to their camp.

The journals of the expedition describe the way Shoshonis dressed. Both men and women wore robes and moccasins, ornaments of seashells, iron arm bands, and leather collars with decorations of dyed porcupine quills. They pierced their ears for jewelry, but not their noses. The Shoshoni created and wore beautiful garments even though they had hard lives and nearly constant hunger.

Cameahwait wanted to go east to hunt buffalo for the winter's food, but he agreed to stay to trade with Lewis, who desperately needed some Shoshoni horses. This was the moment for which Lewis brought Sacagawea on the expedition. The translation chain to buy horses went like this: Lewis spoke English to Labiche, who spoke French to Charbonneau. Charbonneau spoke Hidatsa to Sacagawea. She spoke Shoshoni to Cameahwait. Lewis insisted on getting enough horses and a guide to cross the mountains before winter.

Although the Shoshoni were poor people, they had excellent horses. They were the first tribe in the Northwest to have horses. Their Comanche relatives had brought them north from New Mexico in about 1705. One hundred years

On August 17, 1805, Lewis wrote, "we. . .formed a canopy of one of our large sails and planted some willow brush in the ground to form a shade for the Indians to set under while we spoke to them. . .accordingly about 4pm we called them together and through the medium of Labuish, Charbono and Sah-cah-gar-weah, . .we communicated that [we needed] their horses to transport our baggage. . and that a pilot to conduct us through the mountains was also necessary if we could not descend the river by water." (*Thwaites* 2:362)

later in 1805, Lewis estimated the Shoshoni had about 700 horses, including forty colts and twenty mules. Shoshoni valued the mules at much higher prices than their horses. When the trading ended, the expedition had twenty-seven or twenty-eight horses and one mule.

Cameahwait told Clark that the Salmon River was impossible to navigate, but he explored it anyway. He and his eleven men found that the chief was right. On August 25, the expedition left the Shoshoni camp with horses laden with baggage, heading north, looking for a way to cross the mountains.

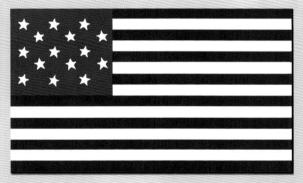

There were seventeen states in the United States of America when Lewis and Clark made their journey. But there were only fifteen stars on the flags the explorers carried. The captains presented this flag to Native American tribes as they met them during the expedition.

Crossing the Lolo Trail

Toby, a Shoshoni elder, became the guide for the expedition when it left the Shoshoni camp. Four of his sons accompanied them, but only one stayed for the trip over the mountains. The expedition went north over very steep land. Some of the horses with heavy packs slipped and rolled down the mountainside, but they survived. Because mountains in the east are so much smaller, men wrote of their amazement of the western terrain. Whitehouse said that the mountains were nearly as "Steep as the roof of a house." At night, temperatures went below freezing. Ordway said that his fingers hurt from the cold.

In a pleasant valley in present–day Monte. They bought eleven more horses and traded seven of their horses for better o. On September 9, 1805, they reached a place they called "Traveler's Rest," rested at Lolo Hot Springs before starting the hardest part of their journey. Torail, but eventually led them out of the brushy canyon where the Lochsa Riverto a dividing ridge where it was easier to travel. (Today a road called Motor hundred years ago, the forest had lots of dead timber, making it very hard toy. Lewis' desk was smashed when the horse carrying it slipped and rolled dowhen it hit a tree. Sergeant Gass wrote that they "proceeded over the most teIt was cold. Men who didn't have socks wrapped rags on their feet to keep the

Few animals lived in the Bitterroot Mouhe Great Plains and lush valleys. (Later, settlements of people forced them inpedition couldn't find game. They were so hungry on the Lolo Trail that theyght. They ate "portable soup" that they did not like. On September 21, all thirty-three of them shared a meal of just a wolf and a couple of birds.

By the time Clark led an advance party into the Nez Perce camp at present-day Weippe, Idaho, all members of the expedition were tired, cold and hungry. Some of the men had problems with their digestive systems and their skin was breaking out. Going over the Bitterroot Mountains proved to be "a bitter crossing." They found there was no easy passage to the Pacific Ocean. The myth of the "Northwest Passage" was not true.

On September 15, 1805, Lewis wrote, "Several horses Sliped and roled down Steep hills. . .the one which Carried my desk & Small trunk Turned over & roled down a mountain for 40 yards & lodged against a tree, broke the Desk the horse escaped and appeared but little hurt." (*Thwaites* 3:67-68)

On September 24, 1805, William Clark wrote, "Capt Lewis [scarcely] able to ride on a jentle horse which was furnished by the chief, Several men So unwell that they were Compelled to lie on the Side of the road." On September 28, he wrote, "our men nearly All Complaining of their bowels, a heaviness of the Stomach. . ." (*Thwaites* 3:87 and 89)

Meeting the Nez Perce

On September 18, 1805, Clark and six hunters went ahead to search for game. They stumbled through a very rough area Clark called Hungry Creek. Then they came onto a lovely plain with Indian lodges in what is now Weippe Prairie, Idaho. Some Indian boys led them to a Nez Perce village where people offered them food. The seven men eagerly ate dried salmon and bread made of camas roots.

The Nez Perce people say that a woman named Watkuweis saved Clark's small advance party from death. Some of the young tribesmen suggested killing the strangers but Watkuweis said that she had been treated well by white men when she was held captive by another tribe in the north. She argued to save them. So the Nez Perce were hospitable and helpful to the Lewis and Clark Expedition.

Clark sent Rueben Field back to tell Lewis that they had met the Nez Perce (also called "Choppunish" Indians). He traveled on to meet an important chief, Twisted Hair. The next day, Clark returned to the first village to meet Lewis and the rest of the expedition. They all ate a lot of the dried salmon and camas roots, but the food did not agree with them, and nearly all of them were sick for more than a week. Clark wrote that Lewis was so sick he could hardly ride a gentle horse that a chief had given him. Several men collapsed on the side of the road because they were so sick. They bought a few dogs to eat, meat that they fortunately found easier to digest. The Nez Perce, who did not eat dogs or horses, found the eating habits of their visitors strange.

Twisted Hair and his sons offered to keep the expedition horses over the winter while they went to the Pacific coast and back. On October 5, they gathered thirty-eight horses, branded them and cut their forelocks in order to identify them the next spring. They buried their saddles. (Lewis' branding iron, found in about 1892, is at the Oregon Historical Society.)

The Nez Perce showed the men how to burn out cottonwood trees to make canoes, a method that took less time than carving them out. On the Clearwater River at a place called "Canoe Camp, " they constructed their canoes. On October 8, they started down the river. The canoe that Gass was steering sprang a leak, split nearly in two, and hung upon a rock. Some of the men could not swim, but were able to get out of the swift water because it was not too deep.

On October 9, Toby and his son left on their horses to return to the Shoshoni Village. They had led the expedition over the hardest part of the trail, receiving no pay for their services. They left without saying goodbye. Maybe they feared going down the river in boats or meeting tribes they didn't know, or maybe they just wanted to go home.

On October 8, 1805, Whitehouse wrote, "as we were descending a rockey rapids. . ., one of the canoes Struck a rock snd wheled round then Struck again and cracked the cane and was near spliting hir in too, throwed the Stearsman over board,. . .Some of the men on board could not Swim." (*Thwaites* 7: 167-8) Gass, the steersman, wrote the same day, "fortunately the water was not more than waist deep, so our lives and baggage were saved." (MacGregor, 136)

To the Pacific Ocean and Back

The thirty-three people could travel faster going downstream with the current of the Clearwater River, which flows into the Snake River at present-day Lewiston, Idaho, and into the Columbia River at present-day Tri-cities, Washington. On the Columbia, the expedition met many different tribes of people. On November 7, Clark wrote of the joy he felt seeing the Pacific Ocean at a distance.

More than a month passed before they got settled for the winter. The north shore of the Columbia turned out to be rocky with little game to eat. So everybody voted on which side of the river they should spend the winter, and crossed to the south side. It was unique that an Indian and a woman—Sacagawea—could vote. Likewise, York voted at a time when blacks were still slaves. This marked a great event in American democracy but, at the time, it was a case of mutual survival.

By Christmas of 1805, they had built a shelter called Fort Clatsop on the Netul River near present-day Astoria, Oregon, several miles from the ocean. It had a big dormitory room for everybody except the captains and the Charbonneau family. They each had private rooms. They built a "salt cairn" at the ocean, a place to boil sea water to get salt to flavor and help preserve the meat from animals they killed.

Sacagawea asked Captain Clark if she could see the "big water" since she had come with them for such a long distance. In January, she and her baby "Pomp" (Clark's nickname for Jean Baptiste) saw the coast.

At Fort Clatsop, the men traded with local Indians, hunted, made extra moccasins for the return trip, and put up with bad weather. It rained every day except six. Sometimes, the rain made their meat rot before they could eat it. It also rotted their buckskin clothes. In addition, the tribes on the ocean had little interest in the poor trade goods that Lewis and Clark's expedition had by this time. These tribes were used to trading with white people who had much more to offer. Unfortunately, several of the men had became ill while they were on the coast. So the leaders decided to leave in March 1806 and return earlier than planned.

Some Nez Perce people traveled west at the same time to meet the Corps of Discovery. Across the Snake River in present-day Oregon, Chief Wearkkoomt and ten men met them on May 3. Days later, they met Twisted Hair. He told them that people found their saddles. He said that all of the saddles and thirty-six horses were in fine shape.

Lewis wrote on Monday, January 6, 1806, "the Indian woman. . .observed that she had traveled a long way with us to see the great waters." (Sacagawea hadn't been to the ocean yet, so the captains granted her wish.) (*Thwaites* 3:314-5)

The Long Camp

The Nez Perce told Lewis and Clark the snow was too high in the mountains to travel, so they made a camp on the Clearwater River at present-day Kamiah, Idaho. This camp is called Camp Choppunish or the Long Camp. They stayed there from May 14 until June 10, 1806. This was the third-longest stay on the trip, after Fort Mandan and Fort Clatsop.

A party of three men, Ordway, Frazer and W[...]on River country for several days. During the trip Frazer traded his razor to [...]mp for two Spanish dollars that she had. These men found the Salmon River co[...]

At the Long Camp, the men gathered the res[...]orse and dog meat, most of the party didn't become sick like they had been [...]. Sacagawea (Clark called her "Janey") often found good, natural green foods, [...] little boy was very sick during the end of May and the first of June. William B[...]he Pacific Ocean. They used a Nez Perce method of healing to cure him. They [...]en into the cold air. His health improved. An older Nez Perce man was c[...]

While waiting for the snow to melt on the m[...]d many new botanical specimens—flowers, trees, bushes and grasses. In fact [...]they brought back to the United States were from present-day Idaho.

The Lewis and Clark Expedition enjoyed a wonderful cultural exchange with the Nez Perce people during their time at the Long Camp. They fished on the Clearwater River, hunted in the surrounding area, and traded goods for food with the Nez Perce. They had some horse races and some foot races with the Nez Perce. They listened to and watched each other's music and dancing.

By the middle of June, the group had gathered all of their horses and tried to cross the mountains. They passed Weippe Prairie, brilliant with blue camas flowers. When they got to the mountains, the snow was too deep and there was no food for their horses. They had to turn back on June 17, the only time that they ever went backwards from their goal. They returned to Weippe. They waited, hoping for Nez Perce guides to arrive to help them cross the mountains. On June 23, three Nez Perce men arrived, and they set out the next day to cross snowy ridges over the Lolo Trail. On June 29, they got to Lolo Hot Springs where everyone enjoyed bathing in the hot water after the cold trek.

At Traveler's Rest where they arrived June 30, they rested and made plans for their return trip. Lewis wanted to explore the Marias River north of the Missouri in present-day Montana. Meanwhile, Clark would take the largest group south to follow the Yellowstone River. It flowed all the way across southern Montana and entered the Missouri near the border of present-day North Dakota. The plan was that Sergeant Ordway and nine men would go with Clark to Three Forks, and down the Jefferson River to the Missouri River in the canoes they had buried at Camp Fortunate the year before. Sergeant Pryor and three men were to ride the horses across the plains and meet an American trader at the Mandan village. Sergeant Gass was to accompany Captain Lewis. Sick men were to portage baggage at the falls.

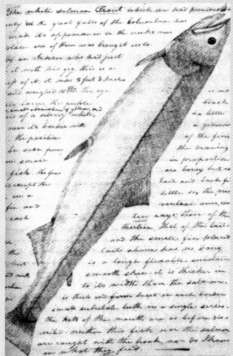

A page from Lewis' diary that includes a drawing of a trout.

On July 4, the Nez Perce guides left them. They split to go their separate ways, but things did not work out the way that the captains planned. The day after Pryor's group left, Indians, perhaps Crows, stole all the horses they were supposed to herd overland. The four men had to kill buffalo and stretch their hides over bent wood to make two "bull boats" to go down the Yellowstone River. They later met Clark's group.

Another band of Indians stole several of Lewis' horses, so Sergeant Gass, Werner and Frazer had to stay with three men packing baggage around the Great Falls. Meanwhile, Captain Lewis, the Fields brothers and Drouillard rode the horses they still had to explore the Marias River area. The four of them camped with eight Piegan Blackfeet Indians near the river. One of the Indians took the Fields brothers' guns and tried to steal Lewis' horses. They fought. Two Indians were killed. Lewis and his men escaped, taking all the horses. Fearing an attack by the Blackfeet, they raced to the Missouri River. It was very lucky that they met up with Gass' party as it was going down the Missouri.

Later, when Lewis and Cruzatte were hunting elk, Cruzatte accidentally shot Lewis in the hip. Cruzatte could not see well and mistook Lewis for an elk. So when they met Clark on August 12, Lewis was lying down in the canoe,

On May 29, 1806, John Ordway wrote, "Frazer got 2 Spanish mill dollars from a squaw for an old razer we expect they got them from the Snake Indians who live near the Spanish country to the South." (*Quaife*, 361) This event occurred at a Nez Perce family camp when Ordway, Frazer and Weiser went to explore the Salmon River twenty miles above the Snake River.

Lewis wrote on June 8, 1806, "several foot races were run this evening between the indians and our men. . .one of them proved as fleet as Drewer and R. Fields, our swiftest runners. . .after dark we had the violin played and danced for the amusement of ourselves and the indians." (Moulton 5:347)

recovering from his wound. It seemed like a miracle that all the different groups who had been so far apart succeeded in meeting each other within days!

Sacagawea, Charbonneau, and their two-and-a-half-year-old boy stayed at the Mandan village. John Colter joined two fur traders and went back up the Missouri River. The rest of the trip down the Missouri River went quickly because they were going with the current. They met American traders who were surprised to see them. No one had heard from them for more than a year and a half. The expedition had gone to the Pacific Ocean and back. They had succeeded in trading with Indians, noting new plants and animals for science, making maps across the Louisiana Purchase, and claiming new lands for the United States.

Lewis and Clark Opened the West

The Lewis and Clark expedition traveled about 8,000 miles in two and one-half years. The only member who died was Sergeant Floyd. They met many different tribes along the way who were interested in trading. They listed many plants and animals that European scientists had not previously known. They opened the way for fur traders, missionaries, and settlers to follow. The land they traveled later became states within the United States. After their voyage, it was clear that there was no easy passage from one waterway to another, especially through the land that would become Idaho.

The land crossing over the Bitterroots was unique. Idaho is the only state today where there is no record of white men's presence before Lewis and Clark entered the area. Neither of the tribes they met in Idaho, the Shoshoni and the Nez Perce, had ever seen white men. Both of these tribes proved essential to the survival and the success of the expedition.

Passing over the Bitterroot Mountains proved very challenging. At 7,373 feet, Lemhi Pass was the highest place that the expedition traveled. The most difficult passage was north of present-day Salmon, Idaho, and on the Lolo Trail. The steep, rocky areas in the Bitterroot Mountains brought cold, fatigue, and hunger to the thirty-three adventurers.

When the streams of the Missouri became too small, they had to abandon travel by boat and get horses. The

Shoshonis provided the horses the Corps of Discovery needed to cross the mountains. The Nez Perce kept those horses all winter and welcomed the party back to the Clearwater River where they stayed about a month. The expedition's third-longest stay was at present-day Kamiah, Idaho, at the Long Camp.

While at the Long Camp, the expedition collected almost a third of its botanical specimens. Plants like the huckleberry, camas, chaparral, syringa (Idaho's state flower), Engleman spruce, and Ponderosa pine were unknown to scientists before Lewis and Clark described them.

In the land that would become Idaho, the Lewis and Clark Expedition experienced many different things. It was the highest, the hardest, the "horsiest," and the hungriest time during the journey. They succeeded, however, because the Shoshoni and the Nez Perce people helped them accomplish their goals.

Sacagawea originally came from Idaho, near the Montana border. She was very helpful to the thirty-one men on the expedition. She knew which natural roots were edible and could find green food and berries to balance their meat diet. Sacagawea carried her baby the whole way without complaint. She retrieved important lost articles once from a sinking boat. She gave her blue beaded belt to trade on the Pacific coast. Her presence kept the men safe, because war parties never included a woman. When tribes saw the Corps of Discovery, they knew it was not a war party because she was there. Sacagawea of Idaho is the most famous American woman. There are more statues and paintings of her than any other woman, and now there is a dollar coin dedicated to her.

Today, the historic trail in Idaho near Salmon and across the northern part of the state remains much as it was when Lewis and Clark were there. The Bitterroot Mountains have not been changed as much as other places. There are very few places left along the trail of Lewis and Clark's long journey where it still looks like it might have 200 years ago. Citizens today have a special chance to preserve the more natural areas of the trail in the Lemhi Pass area and north across the Lolo Trail. The story of the bittersweet passage of the expedition across the northern Rocky Mountains provides dramatic history for our nation.

* * *

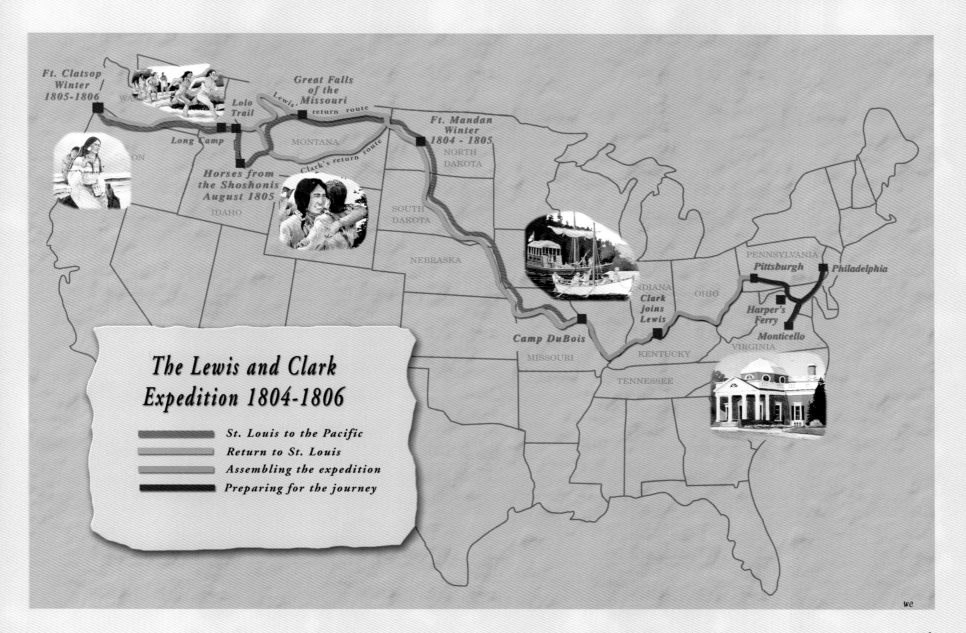

Ft. Clatsop
Winter
1805-1806

WA...

Lolo
Trail

Long Camp

Great Falls
of the
Missouri

Lewis' return route

MONTANA

Clark's return route

Horses from
the Shoshonis
August 1805

IDAHO

Ft. Mandan
Winter
1804 - 1805

NORTH
DAKOTA

SOUTH
DAKOTA

NEBRASKA

PENNSYLVANIA

Pittsburgh

Philadelphia

INDIANA

Clark
joins
Lewis

OHIO

Harper's
Ferry

Camp DuBois

MISSOURI

KENTUCKY

Monticello

VIRGINIA

TENNESSEE

**The Lewis and Clark
Expedition 1804-1806**

St. Louis to the Pacific
Return to St. Louis
Assembling the expedition
Preparing for the journey

wc

GLOSSARY

armaments - guns, powder and weapons

astronomy - the study of stars, used to locate places on earth

biscuit - hard cooked, dry bread that you can keep a long time

blacksmith - a man who works with iron in fire to form useful things like corn mills, horseshoes, moccasin awls, or clothes hooks

botanical - relating to the study of plants

botany - the study of plants

butte - a flat landform that juts above ground; a distinctive hill

cairn - a pile of stones

colt - a young horse still with its mother

confluence - the point where one river runs into another

debris - junk or waste

digestive system - the stomach and gut where food travels through a human or animal

disputed - argued about

encompassing - including or going completely around

estuary - the mouth of a river

ethnology - the study of native people

Euro-Americans - people living in the United States whose ethnic roots are in Europe

expedition - a trip planned for a group with a purpose

fennel - an edible green plant that grew wild in northern Idaho

forelocks - the part of a horse's mane that lies on its face between its ears

keelboat - a type of boat designed with oars and storage to transport men and goods

interpreter - a person who translates one language into another.

Louisiana Purchase - refers to the purchase of land between the Missouri River and the Rocky Mountains, bought by the United States in 1803 from France for $15 million

manufactured - made by men

mares - mother horses

"mess" - a military term for the group of men serving under a sergeant

military discipline -rules of behavior for members of the army, navy, and other military services

moccasin awl - an iron object upon which one can sew moccasins

Monticello - name of President Jefferson's home on a hill in Virginia near Charlottesville

Native Americans - tribal people who lived on the American continent long before white Europeans arrived. Sometimes called Indians.

parchment - strong, tough paper

pirogue - a deep canoe useful to carry men and many goods

pipe tomahawk - a weapon and a smoking devise, made of sharp stone bound to a wooden handle with a carved pipe on it

portage - the carrying of goods around waterfalls

pristine - pure and natural, original condition

procedure - way of doing things

sergeant - a rank in the Army above private and below captain

specimen - plants or animals preserved for scientific reasons

terrain - ground, land, landscape

trek - a walking trip

voyage - trip or expedition

woodsmen - men that are used to the woods, hunting, tracking and finding their way

zoology - the study of animals.

APPENDIX A
Dates of entry of states into the United States prior to 1804:

State	Date	State	Date
Delaware	Dec. 7, 1787	Virginia	June 25, 1788
Pennsylvania	Dec. 12, 1787	New York	July 26, 1788
New Jersey	Dec. 18, 1787	North Carolina	Nov. 21, 1789
Georgia	Jan. 2, 1788	Rhode Island	May 29, 1790
Connecticut	Jan. 9, 1788	Vermont	March 4, 1791
Massachusetts	Feb. 6, 1788	Kentucky	June 1, 1792
Maryland	April 28, 1788	Tennessee	June 1, 1796
South Carolina	May 23, 1788	Ohio	March 1, 1803
New Hampshire	June 21, 1788		[1]

[1]Faragher, John Mack, Buhle, Mari Jo, et al, *Out of Many* (Upper Saddle River, New Jersey; Prentice Hall, 2000, third ed.) A-16.

The fifteen-star flag was created in 1795. It did not change until 1818. Lewis and Clark gave Native Americans fifteen-star flags and told them they now lived in territory belonging to the United States. This message reflected the Louisiana Purchase of 1803. The land west of the Continental Divide (Idaho, Oregon and Washington) was disputed between Great Britain and the United States until 1848.

APPENDIX B
MEMBERS OF THE EXPEDITION
These people went from the Mandan village west to the Pacific Ocean and back ("The Corps of Discovery"):

Captain Meriwether Lewis, U.S. Infantry
Captain William Clark, U.S. Artillery
Sergeant Patrick Gass
Sergeant John Ordway
Sergeant Nathaniel Pryor
Private William Bratton
Private John Collins
Private John Colter (left expedition on its return to Fort Mandan and returned west to become a fur trapper)
Private Peter Cruzatte
Private Joseph Field
Private Reuben Field
Private Robert Frazer
Private George Gibson
Private Silas Goodrich
Private Hugh Hall
Private Thomas Proctor Howard
Private Francois Labiche
Private Jean Baptiste LePage
Private Hugh McNeal
Private John Potts
Private George Shannon
Private John Shields

Private John B. Thompson
Private Peter M. Weiser
Private William Werner
Private Joseph Whitehouse
Private Alexander Hamilton Willard
Private Richard Windsor
George Drouillard, interpreter
York

Died:

Sergeant Charles Floyd, died August 20, 1804, near Sioux City, Iowa, on Missouri River.

These men joined on the Missouri River:

Pierre Dorion, Sr.
Joseph Gravelines
Phillipe Degie

These people joined at Fort Mandan and stayed at Fort Mandan on the return:

Sacagawea
Toussaint Charbonneau
Jean Baptiste Charbonneau ("Pomp)
Jean Baptiste LePage (November 3, 1804 replaced Newman as a permanent member)

Men who were on the first leg of the trip only to the Mandan Village and back to St. Louis:

Corporal John Boley
Corporal John Dame
Corporal Jean Baptiste DeChamps
Corporal John Newman, (court martialed)
Corporal John G. Robertson
Corporal Ebenezer Tuttle
Corporal Richard Warfington
Corporal Isaac White

Private Joseph Barter "La Liberte", (deserted)
Engagé Alexander Carson
Engagé Charles Caugee
Engagé Joseph Collin
Engagé Charles Hebert
Engagé Jean Baptiste LaJeunnesse
Engagé Etienne Malboeuf
Engagé Peter Pinaut
Engagé Paul Primeau
Engagé Francois Rivet
Engagé Pierre Roi
Engagé Roky

BIBLIOGRAPHY

Cutright, Paul Russell, *Lewis & Clark: Pioneering Naturalists* (Lincoln and London: University of Nebraska Press, 1969).

MacGregor, Carol Lynn, *The Journals of Patrick Gass* (Missoula: Mountain Press, 1997).

Moulton, Gary, *Journals of the Lewis & Clark Expedition* (Lincoln and London: University of Nebraska Press, 1986-1999)

Quaife, Milo M., ed. *The Journals of Capt. Meriwether Lewis and Sergeant John Ordway.* (Madison, Wisconsin: The Society, 1916.)

Quiri, Patricia Ryon, *The American Flag,* (New York: Children's Press, 1998).

Thwaites, Rueben Gold, *Original Journals of the Lewis and Clark Expedition* (New York: Arno Press, 1969).

STUDY QUESTIONS

1. Why was the crossing of the Bitterroot Mountains "bitter"? Why was it "sweet"?
2. Describe people on the expedition other than the 'famous five' (Lewis, Clark, Sacagawea, Charbonneau and York).
3. What talents did different individuals bring to the group? What were some of the highlights of the journey to these other members of the exploration party?
4. English spelling did not become standardized until about 1750. What errors can you find in the text quoted directly from Lewis' and Clark's original journals?

**Other books by
Carol MacGregor**

Shoshoni Pony
CAXTON PRESS
ISBN 0-87004-431-1
$15.95

The Journals of Patrick Gass
Mountain Press, 1997

CAXTON PRESS
A DIVISION OF THE CAXTON PRINTERS, LTD.

312 MAIN STREET
CALDWELL, IDAHO 83605

WWW.CAXTONPRESS.COM